Whakaakoranga Kura Tuatahi

THE
Hīkairo Schema
FOR PRIMARY

Culturally Responsive
Teaching and Learning

Matiu Rātima, Jennifer Smith, Angus Macfarlane, Sonja Macfarlane

NZCER PRESS

New Zealand Council for Educational Research
PO Box 3237
Wellington
New Zealand

© NZCER Press, 2020

ISBN 978-1-98-854284-3

This book is not a photocopiable master.

No part of the publication may be copied, stored or communicated in any form by any means (paper or digital), including recording or storing in an electronic retrieval system, without the written permission of the publisher. Education institutions that hold a current licence with Copyright Licensing New Zealand may copy from this book in strict accordance with the terms of the CLNZ Licence. A catalogue record for this book is available from the National Library of New Zealand

Designed by Smartwork Creative Ltd, www.smartworkcreative.co.nz

Distributed by NZCER Distribution Services
PO Box 3237
Wellington
New Zealand
www.nzcer.org.nz

A note on the cover artwork

The cover artwork is the creation of Hikairo Macfarlane. He bears the same name as the famous tipuna, Hikairo, and shares iwi links to Ngāti Rangiwewehi. He attended Hamilton Boys' High School and is enrolled as a scholar at Toihoukura—School of Māori Visual Art and Design at EIT in Gisborne. This is the second schema to which he has artistically contributed. He considered providing the artwork to the Hikairo Schema a privileged assignment. Here is the young Hikairo's portrayal of his artwork:

The intention was to depict the ancestral Hikairo as a leader who cared for the people and their aspirations. He placed huge importance on serving his iwi, Ngāti Rangiwewehi. Hikairo is featured at the base, watching over the learners who receive educational support within the system. At the core is a depiction of "Māori learners succeeding as Māori". The eight patterns surrounding the core are the five Tātaiako competencies along with the three important constructs from the Hikairo Schema—relevance, balance of power, and scaffolding. Teachers and learners face challenges, and these are portrayed by the protractions at each side of Hikairo. Above these protractions are a pair of larger, elaborate wings extending outwards from the centre. These show the tamariki, after overcoming their challenges, soaring towards their next phases of education.

Contents

Preamble	5
Acknowledgements	7
Foreword	9
Motivating and engaging ākonga	11
The model / He rauemi aromatawai	14
How to use this guide	18
Poutama	20
He Poutama: Cultural Competency	22
The Hikairo Schema in practice	23
Huataki—Begin affirmatively	24
Ihi—Demonstrate assertiveness	26
Kotahitanga—Establish inclusion	29
Āwhinatia—Build connections	32
Ira Manaaki—Engender care	35
Rangatiratanga—Enhance meaning	38
Engaging with whānau and hapori	41
Glossary	43
Further useful readings	45
References	46

Preamble

Ka mihi, ka tangi, ka aroha ki ō tātou mate kua hinga, kua ngaro. Ka nui te aroha ki a koutou. Ka huri ki a tātou te hunga ora, arā, tātou e whakapau kaha ana i te ao mātauranga. Nā reira kei te mihi, kei te mihi.

Life in the educational professions has always been fraught with intrigue, and often with ambiguity. How are we to understand the worldviews and learning styles of the diverse cultures that populate today's early childhood centres and schools? What are the origins of these orientations, and what are the most appropriate responses that professionals can offer? How can we assess the effects of our teaching, and what are the implications for learners' outcomes? These questions have stimulated lively and sometimes irascible discussion. Teacher-education programs are charged with the daunting task of preparing the next generation of teachers. However, the extant literature has documented that the majority of teacher-education programs have struggled to effectively prepare teacher candidates with adequate cultural competence to meet the needs of our increasingly diverse population. And while initial teacher education (ITE) is attempting to "get in early", there are literally tens of thousands of experienced teachers and paraprofessionals who are making a clarion call for resources to be made available to the sector. They are calling for resources that would take them closer to a set of new agenda—particularly those that are concerned with better outcomes for Māori learners. To this end, the Hikairo Schema examines the feasibility of integrating many culturally responsive pedagogies into ITE while simultaneously responding to the needs of the numerous practising teachers who constantly express a desire for access to resources that would assist them to be more culturally adept at their craft.

The thinking that led to a decision to do something about this predicament arose out of the relatively constant mismatch between the fixed, sometimes linear, scientific approaches that the evidence-based movement seems to claim, and the pragmatic, workable approach proposed by the world of practice. This book advances the notion that drawing from both approaches would be more robust than either approach would be on its own, and more effective than one approach dominating over the other and builds on the success of the *The Hikairo Schema: Culturally Responsive Teaching and Learning in Early Childhood Settings* (2019). It represents a natural progression from early childhood to primary education and aims to continue to reinforce culturally responsive teaching as a priority for the sector. This version has linked to the "what" of the *The New Zealand Curriculum* (Ministry of Education, 2007). It has served as a reminder to the authors, the research team, and the advisors of the importance of growing awareness of the dynamic and revolving realities of Māori culture, knowledge, and understandings.

The Hikairo Schema for Primary is a good example of culture growing out of the past and functioning in the present, with a vision for the future. Not unlike its predecessor, throughout the text the centrality of relationships is espoused as being critical to primary-school education. In that regard, the reputation of a tribal tupuna provides the basis for six co-existing components of a model that are introduced, described, and explained, to support culturally responsive pedagogies. The research team was keen to offer something that would contribute to the "how" of culturally responsive teaching—in sensible and appetising ways.

E ngā nui o te whakaaro, e ngā pou o te ako, e ngā pūtake o te mārama, e ngā reo, e ngā mana, tēnei te mihi ki a koutou. Anei mātou te kāhui rangahau e whāriki atu nei ki mua i te aroaro o te hunga mātauranga. Hopukina mai, wānangatia, kōrerotia, mahia ki tāu e tika ai. Nā reira, huri noa i te motu, tēnā koutou katoa.

Dr Angus Hikairo Macfarlane
Professor of Māori Research

Acknowledgements

There is always room for optimism when successful educational outcomes for tamariki Māori are on the agenda, but never more so than when teachers are engaged with one another and when culturally responsive practices are taken into account. Fortunately, the New Zealand education system, in more recent times, has rendered high priority to schools keen to work to facilitate the learning and development of their priority learners. Healthy school communities usually identify and practise a set of deeply held cultural values and standards; they also tend to be prepared to communicate by discussing things without too much filtering, and they role model effective methods for dealing with dilemmas impacting on their children's progress. Healthy school communities offer opportunities for children to explore issues with cultural and pedagogical guidance and give ideas for coping with learning and motivational challenges. That said, there remains much room for improvement in the way the schooling system responds to Māori learners' aspirations, and their expectations that the sector provides a context for tamariki "to be Māori". Supplementary resources are an avenue to which teachers may turn, and the Hikairo Schema is one of a number of options that are available— and its development owes recognition to a range of entities and individuals.

The Schema was co-constructed by a number of individuals and groups who are committed to supporting primary and intermediate school teachers, paraprofessionals, and whānau in their work with tamariki in Years 0 to 8. The authors are grateful for the guidance and authority provided by the Advisory Group that was set up to guide and inform the authors of existing models of good practice, as well as identify where there are gaps and lapses—and how these might be filled or addressed. The authors acknowledge the ongoing support of the College of Education, Health and Human Development, the Child Wellbeing Institute, and the Māori Research Laboratory (Te Rū Rangahau) of the University of Canterbury. They are also indebted to the professional colleagues, postgraduate students, and whānau who generously shared their knowledge, insights, and experiences in the sector. A special mention is extended to Margaret Urlich and Nelson Intermediate School for their assistance in the draft and piloting process, and providing a selection of photographs of their beautiful tamariki to enhance the content and aesthetics of this book. Ka nui hoki te mihi ki a Nathan Riki and Nikki Clarke of Breens Intermediate for the photos of their amazing tamariki in action.

Adopting this collaborative approach has been worthwhile and enjoyable. It has also been enabling, because the content that was developed during the co-constructive process has allowed innovative ideas, concrete strategies, and cultural responsiveness to emerge. Consequently, primary and intermediate school contexts will continue to be meaningful settings within which tamariki can flourish, learn, and grow.

Nei rā te owha atu ki a koutou te rōpū whakahaere o tēnei mahi.

Dr Sonja Macfarlane
Practice and Implementation Adviser, Ministry of Education

Foreword

**E ngā reo, e ngā mana, e ngā taniwha o te ao o te mātauranga
Tēnā koutou, tēnā koutou, tēnā koutou katoa.**

Never has there been a greater need for New Zealand schools to recognise, take action, and address inequities of learning outcomes for tamariki Māori. For too long, schools took the approach that tamariki Māori were in deficit—that they lacked competencies and skills to master academic content. Low expectations, poor community relationships, and lack of respect for te reo and tikanga Māori from teachers and principals are now recognised as instrumental in maintaining inequities. This book offers practical strategies for teachers and school communities, to embrace and integrate te reo and tikanga Māori into the daily routines of schooling. The book seeks to help teachers unlock the potential of tamariki. Te reo me ōna tikanga, once seen as impairments to the learning process, are now assets that make learning more meaningful and engaging.

Prejudiced attitudes, embedded in society's view of itself, were once quite normalised and reinforced. It has taken brave Māori educational leadership from discrete facets of the sector, including the authors of this book, to address many of the prevailing imbalances and offer a more positive and affirming vision. Through the dedication and perseverance of great leaders, we now see the values and benefits of embracing a Māori worldview, revitalising te reo rangatira, and encouraging our tamariki Māori to take pride in the ideals that are theirs by way of heritage—language, culture, and identity. When all schools authoritatively adopt a truly bicultural approach to learning and teaching, the sector will see the outcomes that educators are seeking—tamariki reaching their potential.

The Hikairo Schema for Primary is an outstanding book; a resource filled with a suite of practical, evidence-based techniques for teachers, specialist educators, and paraprofessionals to build strong inclusive relationships with students. It offers insights and interpretations of the knowledge, beliefs and values that competent educators hold dear. The Hikairo Schema demonstrates how to make cultural responsivity a reality in classrooms and schools and challenges teachers and school leaders to embark on a bicultural journey.

I am proud to be involved with this publication. I give it my highest endorsement, and I look forward to seeing educators use it to effect change in schools throughout Aotearoa me Te Waipounamu.

Ngā manaakitanga o te runga rawa,

Whetu Cormick
National President, 2019
New Zealand Principals' Federation

> **TŪNGIA TE URURUA KIA TUPU**
> **WHAKARITORITO TE TUPU O TE HARAKEKE**
> *Clear away the overgrown bushes, so that the new flax shoots will spring forth*
>
> — Mead & Grove (2001)

Motivating and engaging ākonga

The Hikairo Schema prioritises six concepts of Māori culture which can benefit both Māori and non-Māori kaiako and ākonga. It will help kaiako create culturally inclusive environments that support achievement by identifying, nurturing, and utilising the strengths of ākonga. Culturally responsive pedagogies anchor practical strategies for teaching and learning. The Hikairo Schema allies with *The New Zealand Curriculum* (Ministry of Education, 2007) (*NZC*), *Tātaiako* (Ministry of Education/New Zealand Teachers Council, 2011), and *Our Code, Our Standards* (Education Council, 2017) to help teachers operationalise core competencies of culturally responsive teaching in the New Zealand context.

NZC articulates a vision for our young people:

> who will work to create an Aotearoa New Zealand in which Māori and Pākehā recognise each other as full Treaty partners, and in which all cultures are valued for the contributions they bring (p. 8)

The Hikairo Schema seeks to empower kaiako to engage in ongoing development and contribution towards this vision by integrating te reo Māori and tikanga into the learning environment, and by holding whanaungatanga as the core of culturally responsive teaching.

Tātaiako (Ministry of Education/New Zealand Teachers Council, 2011) emphasises five cultural competencies for teachers of Māori learners with a central focus on supporting Māori learners to succeed as Māori. This means that Māori definitions of success should be determined in partnership with students, whānau, and community.

Informed by *Tātaiako*, *Our Code Our Standards* (Education Council, 2017) "sets out the high standards for ethical behaviour ... expected of every teacher" (p. ii) in Aotearoa New Zealand. Central to this code is the value of whanaungatanga and commitment to partnership between Māori and Pākehā in accordance with Te Tiriti o Waitangi.

All teachers are committed to their students, and strive to uphold the values, language, and concepts expressed in *NZC*, *Tātaiako*, and *Our Code Our Standards*. However, those who lack understanding of te reo and tikanga Māori may find themselves at a loss as to how they should action these commitments in culturally responsive ways. This is where the Hikairo Schema is intended to empower teachers with practical ways to implement culturally relevant strategies to engage ākonga.

Even though its guiding values and metaphors come from within a Māori worldview, the Hikairo Schema is fundamentally grounded in aroha. Aroha has a very real place in modern Aotearoa New Zealand learning environments, embracing cooperation, understanding, reciprocity, and warmth. The Hikairo Schema's approach to teaching and learning pedagogy has these qualities in abundance and is simultaneously assertive.

The Hikairo Schema provides ideas and themes through which kaiako can centre their practices and relationships, both in and out of the learning context. Those utilising the tool must be willing to critically and honestly examine their attitudes, beliefs, values, and actions. Greater opportunities for learner's success result when kaiako create an atmosphere of acceptance and a culture of care.

Ākonga in Te Pītau Whakarei engage in a Hangarau Matihiko activity, He Whatunga Māhiti, (Networking) which teaches computational thinking as a 21st-century skill.

Nā Fiona Matapo

The history of Hikairo

The inspiration for the Hikairo Schema is rooted in Māori history; so named because of the way a resolution was reached through mediation following intertribal encounters on Mokoia Island in 1823. Stafford (1967) documented that the Ngāti Rangiwewehi chief, Hikairo[1], intervened with such mana and influence that the illustrious leaders of the day declared that aggression should make way for order. On this occasion, Hikairo's assertive dialogue, fundamental assurances, and simple sincerity brought about a change of attitude and behaviour. Hikairo's inspiration is alive in this guide.

1 The reference to Hikairo (the ancestor) for educational enrichment was originally sanctioned by kaumātua Hami Hahunga, on behalf of Ngāti Rangiwewehi, in a memorandum dated 24 September 1997.

The model

The Hikairo Schema is composed of six co-existing components that, when employed in practice, foster teaching and learning strategies which are inclusive, reciprocal, and collaborative in nature. These dimensions work together to provide insights to incorporating Māori culture and language into teaching, and to developing culturally responsive paradigms both for guiding learning and for supporting teacher development

He rauemi aromatawai[2]

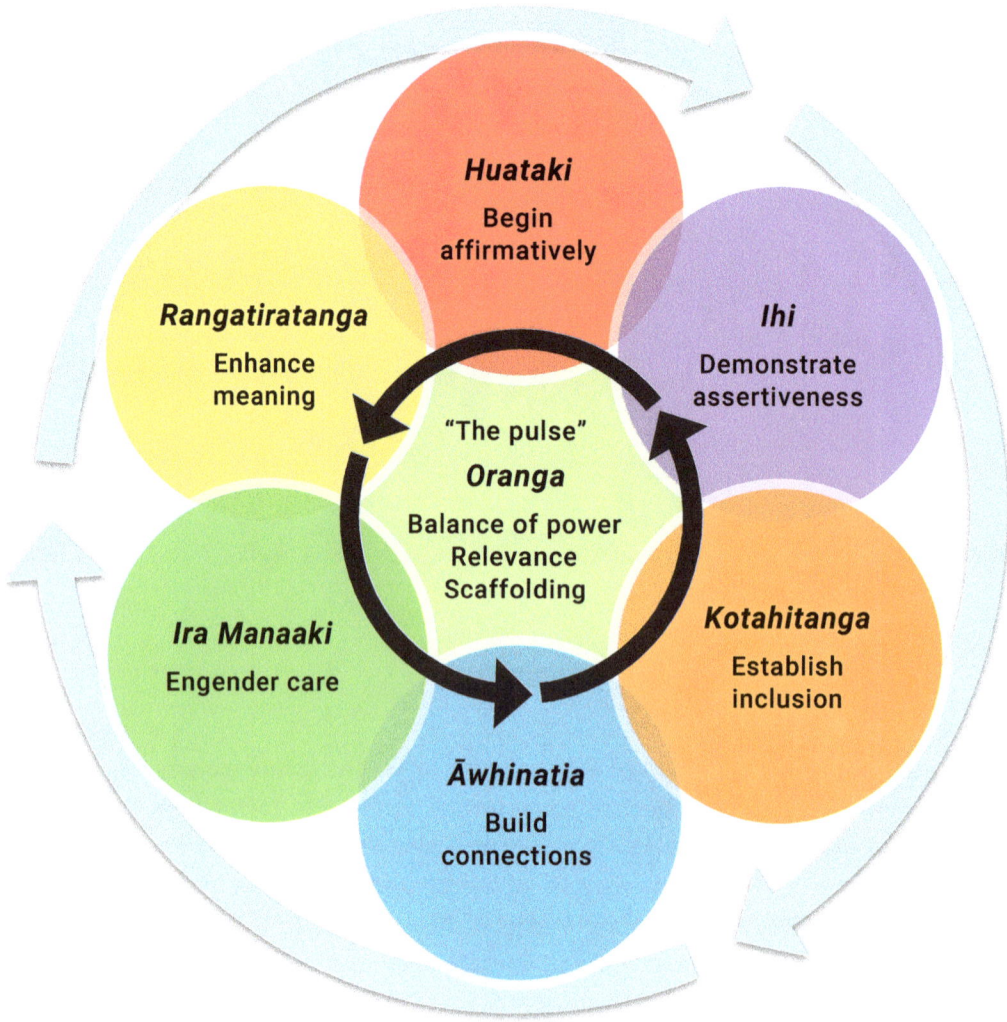

---

[2] He Rauemi Aromatawai aligns with Macfarlane's (2004) *Educultural Wheel,* on the basis of which the present model has been developed in the light of research discussed in Macfarlane (2005) and Macfarlane, Macfarlane and Webber (2015).

At the core of the Hikairo Schema is the pulse—the set of principles that draws life from, and breathes life into, each of the other six components of the model. The three core principles of the schema are **relevance**, **balance of power**, and **scaffolding**. As kaiako work through each of the outer six components, their teaching, pedagogy, and the learning environment should model these three key principles.

Relevance. Align learning with the values of ākonga, as well as their cultural and personal identities.

Achieving cultural relevance is a driving factor in motivating ākonga from cultures different to the dominant discourse. Relevance is continuous with creating culturally safe environments. Enhancing the cultural capacity of learning environments increases the viability of learning contexts and also closes culture and value gaps. Strategies include developing a sense of community, organising the programme and the physical setting so that the culture of the learner is present, and forming experiences that help ākonga to understand their physical and social environments—and themselves—while enhancing mana, and showing respect and care for the world and its people.

Balance of Power. Enhance ako through co-constructing learning contexts (Glasser 1992, Pere 1982). All learners take part in experiences grounded in mutual care, trust, and respect.

Ākonga must build competence and confidence for leadership, for autonomy, and for engaging others in respectful, meaningful relationships. Experiences are collaborative undertakings, co-led by kaiako, ākonga, and whānau. Learning environments foster productive and supportive relationships when cultures are visible and valued. Strategies for balancing power include: establishing cooperative working teams; discussing, negotiating, and agreeing on appropriate behaviours for the classroom context; and, engaging in open-ended dialogue between and amongst kaiako, ākonga, and whānau.

Scaffolding. Ensure that successful outcomes are within the grasp of learners—while providing any necessary resources and support to promote learning.

Modern teaching pedagogies promote learning experiences that are specific, child-centred, credit-based, and at an appropriate level of challenge. Scaffolding supports ākonga by engaging them with successful learning outcomes that are mana enhancing. Strategies include providing clear feedback which promotes confidence and self-efficacy, and designing tasks which offer opportunities to be successful while also extending capacities.

Primary education can be busy and multifaceted. Learning interactions are oftentimes challenging, both emotionally and physically. Nevertheless, the strengthening of the oranga of everyone involved rewards the effort put into happy, caring, and energetic learning environments. The rest of this guide offers a programme designed to help teachers focus on and build cultural capacity within their learning spaces.

Each component invites the assessment of achievements, either through self-assessment or peer-supported. Ask a colleague to observe and comment on your interactions and practices with ākonga and whānau, kaiako, and other members of the community. Use colleagues' experience to build culturally responsive skills and competencies.

Use the at the end of the guide to frame conversations about the development of your cultural competencies.

The Hikairo Schema is useful for providing evidence towards the Education Council's *Our Code, Our Standards* (2017) (see also the inside front cover of this book). School leaders can facilitate discussion around appropriate self-review questions, focusing activities, and outcomes. Suggested self-review questions are included, but these can be revised to better fit kaiako focus and context. For example, the following reflective questions were created to relate to *Our Code, Our Standards*, and the aspects of oranga.

Relevance

What features of a primary classroom and/or whole-school environment help children and whānau feel that this is a place where they belong? (See 2.3 & 3.3 in Education Council (2017), pp. 10, 12.)

How do kaiako recognise and value the, heritage, identities, languages, and cultures of all children? (See 2.3 & 3.3 in Education Council (2017), pp. 10, 12.)

Balance of Power

In what ways do kaiako support children to contribute to curriculum decision making? (See "Learning-focused culture" in Education Council (2017), p. 20.)

How might kaiako strengthen children's self-efficacy and sense of self-worth?

How does the curriculum provide genuine opportunities for children to make choices and develop independence? (See "Learning-focused culture" in Education Council (2017), p. 20.)

Scaffolding

How effectively does the curriculum provide for the interests, strengths, abilities, and preferences of all children and support them to build positive learner identities? (See "Design for learning" in Education Council (2017), p. 20.)

How might kaiako make thoughtful decisions based on theoretical and practical aspects of teaching? (See "Teaching" in Education Council (2017), p. 20.).

How to use this guide

This guide is designed to provide practical advice and opportunities to reflect on what it means to teach in culturally responsive ways. It is intended to be applied in a flexible and empowering way to inspire teachers to broaden and deepen the culture of care within their learning environments.

For those of us within the teaching profession—including individual kaiako, teaching teams, departments, whole-school groups, or kāhui ako—who wish to engage in culturally responsive teaching, there is practical advice for day-to-day practice. The hope is that the suggestions will stimulate thinking, lead to action, and provide some confidence to experiment with different ways of approaching teaching.

For those of us who lead or employ teachers, such as principals, senior managers, and boards of trustees, the book will stimulate fresh ideas for engaging ākonga and for having conversations with teachers about professional development, teaching pedagogy, and school culture.

For those entering the profession, the book supports teacher educators to better prepare student teachers both for the diversity of the New Zealand classroom and for supporting and respecting the cultures of their students.

There are six components in the Hikairo Schema.

1. Huataki—Begin affirmatively.
2. Ihi—Demonstrate assertiveness.
3. Kotahitanga—Establish inclusion.
4. Āwhinatia—Build connections.
5. Ira Manaaki—Engender care.
6. Rangatiratanga—Enhance meaning.

Busy individuals and groups should feel free to focus on one or more of the components for as long as they need to and in a cyclic and reiterative way. The work is important, but there is no need to rush. For example, one of the components might be selected as the focus for a teaching and inquiry cycle for a term or longer. There is a self-reflection tool—Poutama (p. 22)—to be used in conjunction with each component as a guide to gauge progress. There are also sections for Engaging Whānau, a Glossary, and Additional Readings following each component and a reference list to show the whakapapa of evidence-based thinking underpinning the Schema.

How to use the components

Once you have looked through the guide, there may be a component that speaks to you and what you want to achieve with your learners. Start there. For this example, we will start at the most obvious place: Huataki—Begin affirmatively.

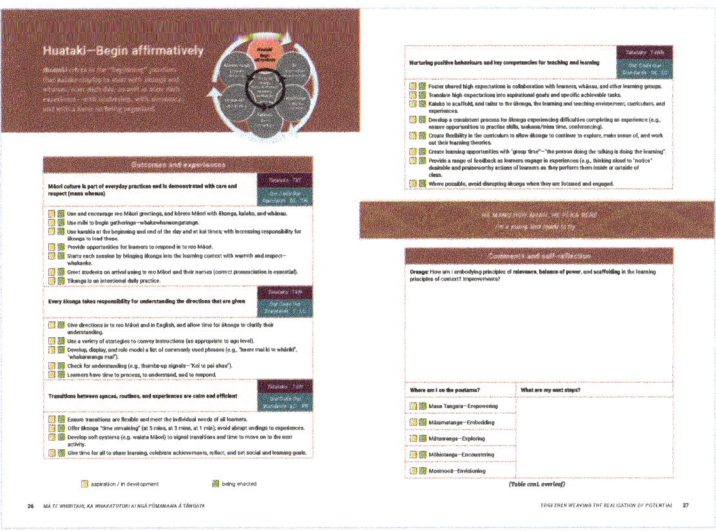

Huataki—Begin affirmatively

Huataki refers to the "beginning" practices that kaiako employ to start with ākonga and in some cases with whānau—to start each day, as well as start each learning block, with leadership, with assurance, and with a focus on being organised.

Take a moment to think—is this what your learning environment is providing for every child? The guide lists examples of what teachers are already doing to make their akomanga more culturally responsive and relevant to their learners. On the left side of each example are two boxes for you to indicate where you are at with each suggestion. If this is an aspiration or is in development, tick the left, yellow box. If this is being enacted already tick the right, green box. If this is not a priority or you don't understand the suggestion leave it blank for now and return to it later. At the top right are codes to indicate the links to *Our Code Our Standards* (Education Council, 2017) and to *Tātaiako* (Ministry of Education/New Zealand Teachers Council, 2011) so all kaiako can see the connections with the cultural competencies and standards endorsed by the Education Council. There is space in each box for you to add culturally responsive actions that you engage in which are not already listed.

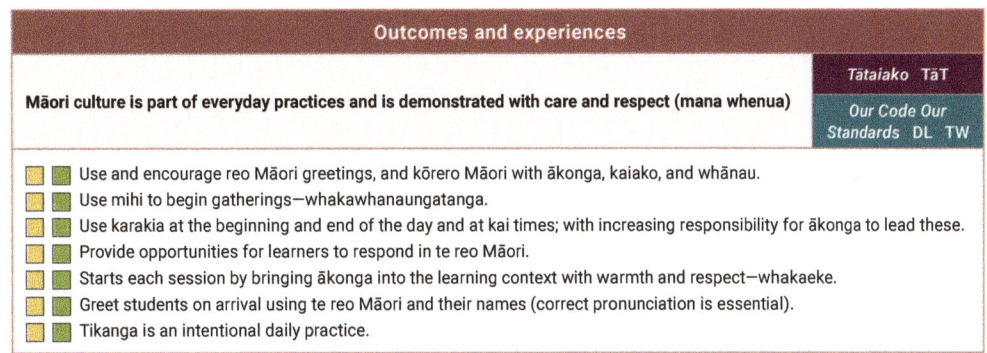

Poutama

Teachers are encouraged to use the Poutama (see p. 22) while they reflect in Oranga. Reflect on how you're embodying principles of relevance, the balance of power, and scaffolding in the learning context. How could this be improved? Student voice may be useful in this section to gauge how it is working for all learners in your space. Use the Poutama to aid in identifying next steps for your teaching.

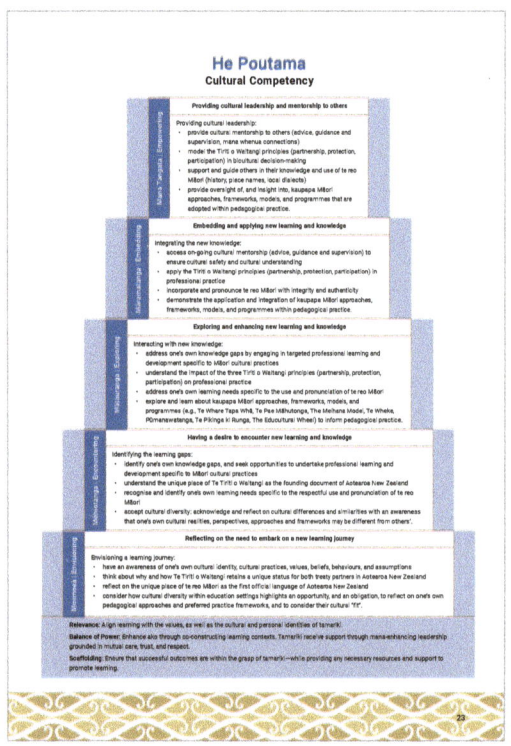 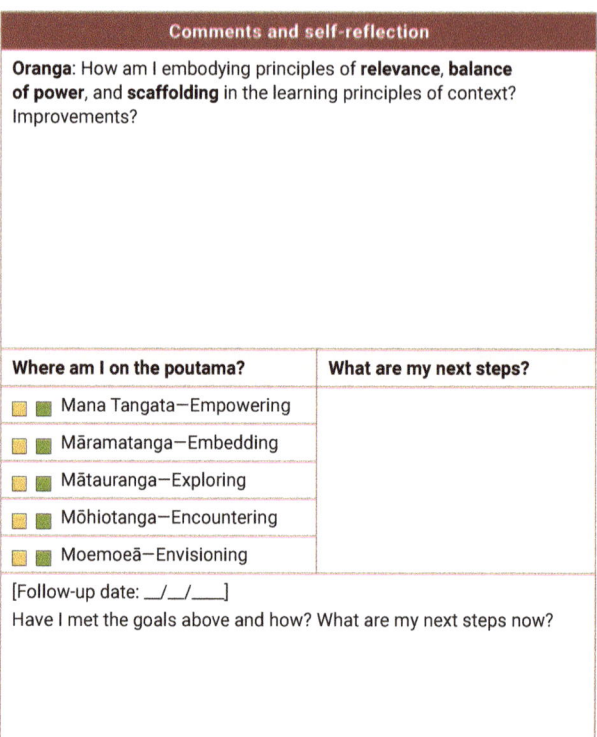

Additional readings

Additional readings have also been added at the bottom of each page. You may choose to use them as jigsaw readings at a team meeting or as pre-readings to share back in inquiry groupings. If you focus on one component for longer than one or two terms, there are more readings in the reference list at the back of the guide to further supplement your professional development.

Revisit any section as often as you like. Once you feel you have reached the top of the poutama—Mana Tangata / Empowering—you are ready to move on. Creating culturally responsive and safe environments will always have an element of revision. No matter where on our journey we are, there will be many more ways to deepen our commitment to engaging all learners

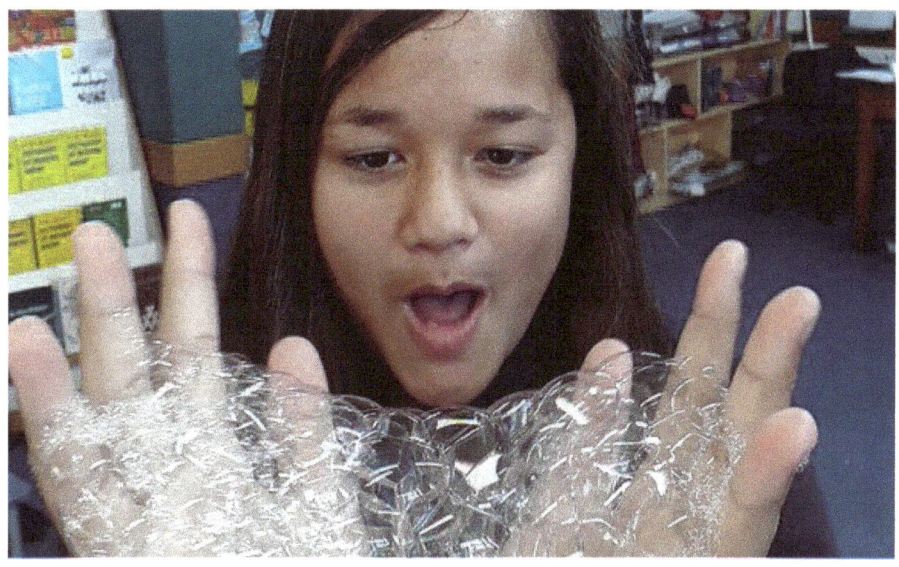

He Poutama
Cultural Competency

Mana Tangata | Empowering
Providing cultural leadership and mentorship to others

Providing cultural leadership:
- provide cultural mentorship to others (advice, guidance and supervision, mana whenua connections)
- model the Tiriti o Waitangi principles (partnership, protection, participation) in bicultural decision-making
- support and guide others in their knowledge and use of te reo Māori (history, place names, local dialects)
- provide oversight of, and insight into, kaupapa Māori approaches, frameworks, models, and programmes that are adopted within pedagogical practice.

Māramatanga | Embedding
Embedding and applying new learning and knowledge

Integrating the new knowledge:
- access on-going cultural mentorship (advice, guidance and supervision) to ensure cultural safety and cultural understanding
- apply the Tiriti o Waitangi principles (partnership, protection, participation) in professional practice
- incorporate and pronounce te reo Māori with integrity and authenticity
- demonstrate the application and integration of kaupapa Māori approaches, frameworks, models, and programmes within pedagogical practice.

Mātauranga | Exploring
Exploring and enhancing new learning and knowledge

Interacting with new knowledge:
- address one's own knowledge gaps by engaging in targeted professional learning and development specific to Māori cultural practices
- understand the impact of the three Tiriti o Waitangi principles (partnership, protection, participation) on professional practice
- address one's own learning needs specific to the use and pronunciation of te reo Māori
- explore and learn about kaupapa Māori approaches, frameworks, models, and programmes (e.g., Te Whare Tapa Whā, Te Pae Māhutonga, The Meihana Model, Te Wheke, Pūmanawatanga, Te Pikinga ki Runga, The Educultural Wheel) to inform pedagogical practice.

Mōhiotanga | Encountering
Having a desire to encounter new learning and knowledge

Identifying the learning gaps:
- identify one's own knowledge gaps, and seek opportunities to undertake professional learning and development specific to Māori cultural practices
- understand the unique place of Te Tiriti o Waitangi as the founding document of Aotearoa New Zealand
- recognise and identify one's own learning needs specific to the respectful use and pronunciation of te reo Māori
- accept cultural diversity: acknowledge and reflect on cultural differences and similarities with an awareness that one's own cultural realities, perspectives, approaches and frameworks may be different from others'.

Moemoeā | Envisioning
Reflecting on the need to embark on a new learning journey

Envisioning a learning journey:
- have an awareness of one's own cultural identity, cultural practices, values, beliefs, behaviours, and assumptions
- think about why and how Te Tiriti o Waitangi retains a unique status for both treaty partners in Aotearoa New Zealand
- reflect on the unique place of te reo Māori as the first official language of Aotearoa New Zealand
- consider how cultural diversity within education settings highlights an opportunity, and an obligation, to reflect on one's own pedagogical approaches and preferred practice frameworks, and to consider their cultural "fit".

Relevance: Align learning with the values, as well as the cultural and personal identities of tamariki.

Balance of Power: Enhance ako through co-constructing learning contexts. Tamariki receive support through mana-enhancing leadership grounded in mutual care, trust, and respect.

Scaffolding: Ensure that successful outcomes are within the grasp of tamariki—while providing any necessary resources and support to promote learning.

The Hikairo Schema in practice

The Hikairo Schema in Years 1–8

Our kaiako attended seminars, read widely, and had learning conversations around culturally responsive teaching and learning to improve student learning. We were keen to get a deeper knowledge of the Schema, relating it to *NZC*, *Te Marautanga o Aotearoa* (Ministry of Education, 2008), *Our Code Our Standards* (Education Council, 2017), *Tātaiako* (Ministry of Education, 2011), *School Evaluation Indicators* (Education Review Office, 2016), and wider research readings available.

Collaboratively, we workshopped the Schema, unpacking components and viewing how it provided a Māori lens to assist reflection on our personal pedagogy. Booklets were created. Teachers chose the component they wanted to be observed on by a peer.

Ākonga were encouraged to contribute to how they viewed the learning environment in each component focused on. This provided "student voice" and feedback to teachers and, along with teacher self reflection and peer observation, rich data was gathered for kaiako learning conversations. New learning, undoing of learning, and teacher next steps ensued.

The Hikairo Schema has developed a school culture focused on teacher and student relationships to improve teaching and learning. Teachers choose which component they will focus on according on the needs of students. They self-reflect on their practice and how effective their relationships with ākonga are in developing the learning dispositions of all students.

Margaret Urlich, Anthony de Thierry
Senior Leaders, Nelson Intermediate

Huataki—Begin affirmatively

Huataki refers to the "beginning" practices that kaiako employ to start with ākonga and whānau, start each day, as well as start each experience—with leadership, with assurance, and with a focus on being organised.

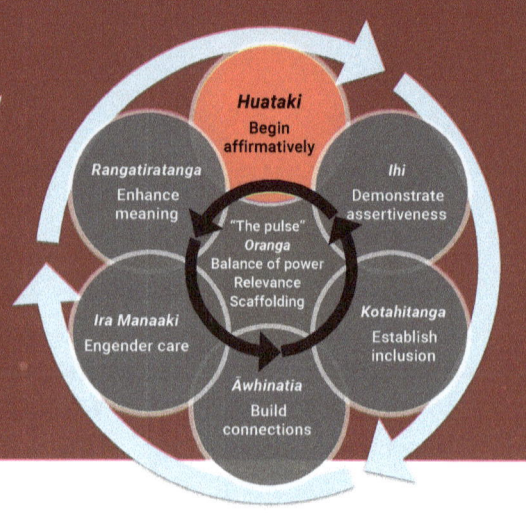

Outcomes and experiences

Māori culture is part of everyday practices and is demonstrated with care and respect (mana whenua)	**Tātaiako TaT**
	Our Code Our Standards DL TW

- ☐ ☐ Use and encourage reo Māori greetings, and kōrero Māori with ākonga, kaiako, and whānau.
- ☐ ☐ Use mihi to begin gatherings—whakawhanaungatanga.
- ☐ ☐ Use karakia at the beginning and end of the day and at kai times; with increasing responsibility for ākonga to lead these.
- ☐ ☐ Provide opportunities for learners to respond in te reo Māori.
- ☐ ☐ Starts each session by bringing ākonga into the learning context with warmth and respect—whakaeke.
- ☐ ☐ Greet students on arrival using te reo Māori and their names (correct pronunciation is essential).
- ☐ ☐ Tikanga is an intentional daily practice.

Every ākonga takes responsibility for understanding the directions that are given	**Tātaiako TaW**
	Our Code Our Standards T LC

- ☐ ☐ Give directions in te reo Māori and in English, and allow time for ākonga to clarify their understanding.
- ☐ ☐ Use a variety of strategies to convey instructions (as appropriate to age level).
- ☐ ☐ Develop, display, and role model a list of commonly used phrases (e.g., "haere mai ki te whāriki", "whakararanga mai").
- ☐ ☐ Check for understanding (e.g., thumbs-up signals—"Kei te pai ahau").
- ☐ ☐ Learners have time to process, to understand, and to respond.

Transitions between spaces, routines, and experiences are calm and efficient	**Tātaiako TaW**
	Our Code Our Standards LC PR

- ☐ ☐ Ensure transitions are flexible and meet the individual needs of all learners.
- ☐ ☐ Offer ākonga "time remaining" (at 5 mins, at 3 mins, at 1 min); avoid abrupt endings to experiences.
- ☐ ☐ Develop soft systems (e.g. waiata Māori) to signal transitions and time to move on to the next activity.
- ☐ ☐ Give time for all to share learning, celebrate achievements, reflect, and set social and learning goals.

☐ aspiration / in development   ☐ being enacted

Nurturing positive behaviours and key competencies for teaching and learning	Tātaiako TāWh
	Our Code Our Standards DL LC

- ☐ ☐ Foster shared high expectations in collaboration with learners, whānau, and other learning groups.
- ☐ ☐ Translate high expectations into aspirational goals and specific achievable tasks.
- ☐ ☐ Kaiako to scaffold, and tailor to the ākonga, the learning and teaching environment, curriculum, and experiences.
- ☐ ☐ Develop a consistent process for ākonga experiencing difficulties completing an experience (e.g., ensure opportunities to practise skills, tuakana/teina time, conferencing).
- ☐ ☐ Create flexibility in the curriculum to allow ākonga to continue to explore, make sense of, and work out their learning theories.
- ☐ ☐ Create learning opportunities with "group time"—"the person doing the talking is doing the learning".
- ☐ ☐ Provide a range of feedback as learners engage in experiences (e.g., thinking aloud to "notice" desirable and praiseworthy actions of learners as they perform them inside or outside of class.
- ☐ ☐ Where possible, avoid disrupting ākonga when they are focused and engaged.

HE MANU HOU AHAU, HE PĪ KA RERE
I'm a young bird ready to fly

Comments and self-reflection

Oranga: How am I embodying principles of **relevance**, **balance of power**, and **scaffolding** in the learning principles of context? Improvements?

Where am I on the poutama?	What are my next steps?
☐ ☐ Mana Tangata—Empowering	
☐ ☐ Māramatanga—Embedding	
☐ ☐ Mātauranga—Exploring	
☐ ☐ Mōhiotanga—Encountering	
☐ ☐ Moemoeā—Envisioning	

(Table cont. overleaf)

TOGETHER WEAVING THE REALISATION OF POTENTIAL

(Table cont. from previous page)

[Follow-up date: __/__/____] Have I met the goals above and how? What are my next steps now?
Additional readings Alton-Lee, A. (2003). *Quality teaching for diverse students in schooling: Best evidence synthesis.* Wellington: Ministry of Education. Macfarlane, S., & Macfarlane, A. (2019) Indigenous and sociocultural imperatives for educational practice. In A. Camp (ed.), *Education studies in Aotearoa: Key disciplines and emerging directions* (pp 9 – 24). Wellington: NZCER Press. Smith, C., & Laslett, R. (2002). *Effective classroom management: A teacher's guide.* Taylor and Francis.

Ihi—Demonstrate assertiveness

Ihi refers to the ability to have a structured and consistent approach to teaching practices. Focus on leading with assertiveness and warmth. There is astute planning and confidence in building and supporting key competencies through use of mana enhancing and restorative practices. The kaiako models and teaches tikanga and key competencies that are appropriate for all learning contexts.

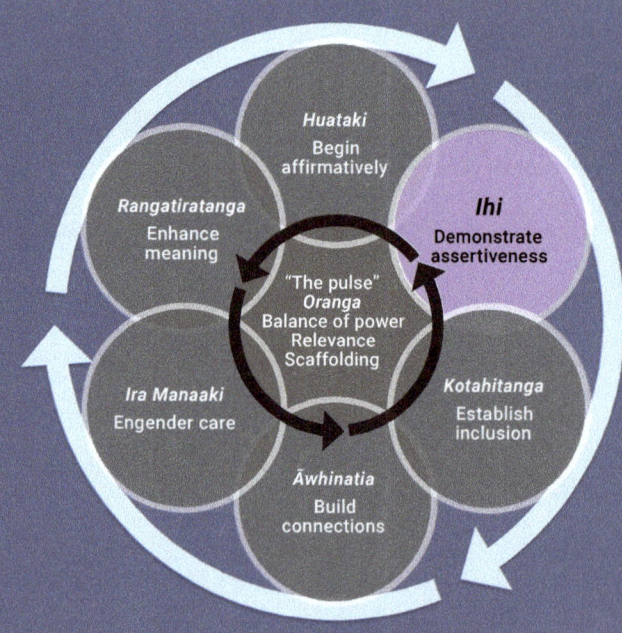

Outcomes and experiences

	Tātaiako TāW
Learning is co-constructed with ākonga and whānau	Our Code Our Standards TW DL

- ☐ ☐ Build confidence for inquiry by creating opportunities for a variety of different experiences, and encouraging curiosity and wonder.
- ☐ ☐ Work alongside and engage learners at their eye-level—kanohi ki te kanohi.
- ☐ ☐ Create learning environments that support and role model ako and tuakana–teina relationships.
- ☐ ☐ Next steps of learning are constructed with whānau and the learner.
- ☐ ☐ Ensure everyone—kaiako, tauira, whānau—knows their responsibilities (tikanga) in the learning environment.
- ☐ ☐ A shared understandings "treaty" is designed, linked to school-wide values and implemented by the learner and kaiako. It is referenced as part of celebrated achievements.
- ☐ ☐ Engage whānau in fun ways that reflect school values (e.g., healthy kai hākari, ki-ō-rahi tournament, mau rākau club, kapa haka performance).

Key competencies are supported in ways that ākonga understand	**Tātaiako** TāA TāM
	Our Code Our Standards T

- ☐ ☐ Use multiple modes to help convey meaning (e.g., texts, visuals, hand gestures, explanations).
- ☐ ☐ Positive social behaviours and key competencies are taught, pulled apart for examination, practised through role-play, and modelled. They are revisited frequently.
- ☐ ☐ Develop positive mindset attitudes—learning from mistakes and focusing on the potential for growth over time.
- ☐ ☐ Celebrate successes of all kinds, not just sport or academic—whakanuia.
- ☐ ☐ Support the building of key competencies with mana, aroha, and manaaki.
- ☐ ☐ Guided tuakana–teina time for social, emotional, and problem-solving skills in context.
- ☐ ☐ Use restorative (whakatika) approaches to guide tamariki towards fixing relationships, problem-solving, and decision making.

Key competencies are developed by setting reasonable and realistic goals	**Tātaiako** TāW TāA
	Our Code Our Standards T

- ☐ ☐ Give positive frequent feedback when ākonga make good decisions.
- ☐ ☐ Set fair and genuine goals—whāinga pai.
- ☐ ☐ Develop home and school partnerships to support goals outside school time.
- ☐ ☐ Celebrate every step of the learning journey, including mistakes.
- ☐ ☐ Celebrate good decision making, both small and big.
- ☐ ☐ Give constructive criticism in mana-enhancing ways.

KAUA E MATE WHEKE, ME MATE URUROA
Don't give up as the octopus does, be assertive like the hammerhead shark

Comments and self-reflection

Oranga: How am I embodying principles of **relevance**, **balance of power**, and **scaffolding** in the learning principles of context? Improvements?

(Table cont. overleaf)

(Table cont. from previous page)

Where am I on the poutama?	What are my next steps?
☐ ☐ Mana Tangata—Empowering	
☐ ☐ Māramatanga—Embedding	
☐ ☐ Mātauranga—Exploring	
☐ ☐ Mōhiotanga—Encountering	
☐ ☐ Moemoeā—Envisioning	

[Follow-up date: __/__/___]
Have I met the goals above and how? What are my next steps now?

Additional readings

Savage, C., Macfarlane, S., Macfarlane, A., Fickel, L., & Te Hemi, H. (2014). Huakina mai: A kaupapa Māori approach to relationship and behaviour support. *Australian Journal of Indigenous Education, 43*(2), 165–174. https://doi.org/10.1017/jie.2014.23

Sleeter, C. E. (2012). Confronting the marginalization of culturally responsive pedagogy. *Urban Education, 47*(3), 562–584. https://doi.org/10.1177/0042085911431472

Kotahitanga—Establish inclusion

Kotahitanga refers to working together respectfully; a feeling of connection and team unity. Focus on fostering inclusion and respectful collaboration. Emphasise principles and practices that contribute to the collective and supportive learning environment (e.g., cooperative learning, tuakana–teina, ako, and peer-learning).

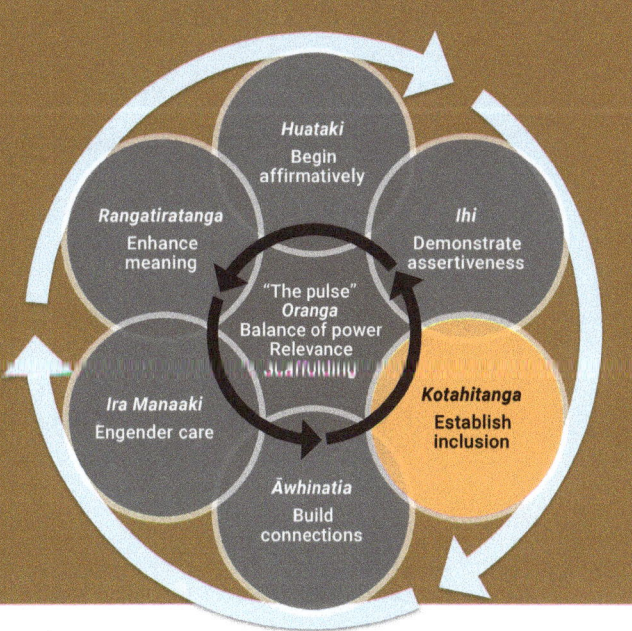

Outcomes and experiences

Learners' cultural values are incorporated into planning, delivery, and documentation

Tātaiako TāT
Our Code Our Standards T DL

- ☐ ☐ Use te reo Māori and encourage all ākonga to speak Māori and share the Māori they know.
- ☐ ☐ Use spoken and written examples of te reo Māori and other languages.
- ☐ ☐ Learn the cultural background of all ākonga, and celebrate and share cultural differences.
- ☐ ☐ Communications, such as newsletters, utilise te reo, are informal, warm, succinct, and frequent.
- ☐ ☐ Plan for the regular inclusion of Māori concepts and contexts within teaching.
- ☐ ☐ Schedule time for ākonga to lead inquiry and learning about one another's cultures.
- ☐ ☐ Honour the cultural backgrounds of learners by including whānau and encouraging the sharing of learner home languages, backgrounds, and practices. Seek input from whānau about what is appropriate.
- ☐ ☐ Connect to local hapori such as the marae. Make meaning of whakapapa through pepeha/mihimihi. Kaiako and ākonga should know the pepeha of the local iwi and marae. Invite ākonga to share their own pepeha/mihimihi, and know about the pepeha of classmates.
- ☐ ☐ Strive to understand your own culture and how this shapes your assumptions about learning.

The inclusive and respectful learning environment engenders trust and cooperation amongst ākonga and kaiako

Tātaiako TāM
Our Code Our Standards PR LC

- ☐ ☐ Make an explicit commitment to show fairness to each learner.
- ☐ ☐ Collaborate with learners and whānau in conversations that focus on and define the kaupapa of the teaching and learning environment.
- ☐ ☐ Create opportunities for ākonga to learn the culture of their peers.
- ☐ ☐ Show sincerity by knowing the iwi/hapū/waka of the learner and something about those iwi (e.g., location, rangatira, history).
- ☐ ☐ Seek advice from those with cultural knowledge.
- ☐ ☐ Where appropriate, share own/personal experiences.
- ☐ ☐ Learning intentions are understood so all ākonga know the "why" of their learning where necessary.
- ☐ ☐ Tuakana–teina/think pair share ideas with peers before asking for answers. Ask buddies to share back their peers' ideas.

Transitions between routines and experiences are calm and efficient	Tātaiako TāA
	Our Code Our Standards T TW

- ☐ ☐ Draw on Māori waiata, whakataukī, and pūrākau to transition between learning activities or experiences.
- ☐ ☐ Tikanga is used to indicate beginning, middle, and end of a learning cycle or activity, and is visible, routine, and underpins practice (e.g., karakia and waiata at the beginning and end of the day).
- ☐ ☐ Avoid interrupting ākonga when they are on a roll. Give 5-minute, 3-minute, and 1-minute warnings before winding up an activity or transitioning to a new one.
- ☐ ☐ Plan for various kinds of learning dynamics (e.g., learner-directed, teacher-directed, and collaborative learning).

Values and identity are encouraged, modelled, and explored	Tātaiako TāT
	Our Code Our Standards TW LC

- ☐ ☐ Invite Māori role models, kaumātua and kuia into the learning environment.
- ☐ ☐ Use local place-based knowledge to connect the curriculum to the lived worlds of ākonga and te ao Māori.
- ☐ ☐ Use Aotearoa New Zealand contexts for learning.
- ☐ ☐ Model an understanding of one's own culture, a positive view of world cultures, and an interest in learning about diversity.
- ☐ ☐ Link learning to local, national, and global events that are relevant to the lives of ākonga and the Māori world.
- ☐ ☐ Te Tiriti o Waitangi evident in school philosophy, policies, planning, curriculum documentation, and physical environment.
- ☐ ☐ Resources are used that reflect a range of perspectives and that create open discussions to celebrate differences and similarities.
- ☐ ☐ Be active/visible in the community (kanohi kitea).

WHAKAPŪPŪTIA MAI O MĀNUKA, KIA KORE AI E WHATI
Bind together the branches of the mānuka so that they will not break.

Comments and self-reflection

Oranga: How am I embodying principles of **relevance**, **balance of power**, and **scaffolding** in the learning context? Improvements?

Where am I on the poutama?	What are my next steps?
☐ ☐ Mana Tangata—Empowering	
☐ ☐ Māramatanga—Embedding	
☐ ☐ Mātauranga—Exploring	
☐ ☐ Mōhiotanga—Encountering	
☐ ☐ Moemoeā—Envisioning	

[Follow-up date: __/__/____]

Have I met the goals above and how? What are my next steps now?

Additional readings

Clarke, T., Macfarlane, S., & Macfarlane, A. (2018). Integrating indigenous Māori frameworks to ignite understandings within initial teacher education—and beyond. In P. Whitinui, M. a. d. C. Rodríguez, & O. McIvor (Eds.), *Promising practices in indigenous teacher education* (pp. 71–85). Singapore: Springer.

Penetito, W. (2009). Place-based education: Catering for curriculum, culture and community. *New Zealand Annual Review of Education, 18*, 529.

Āwhinatia— Build connections

Āwhinatia refers to reducing or eliminating disjointedness, employing the art of "with-it-ness" (see Kounin, 1977), and staying on track with connectedness, smoothness, and momentum. Inform planning by drawing on strengths, interests, and your knowledge of the learner. Mana-enhancing systems are built on a strong foundation of whanaungatanga. This base means that teacher, student, and whānau are accountable to one another for the learner's progress.

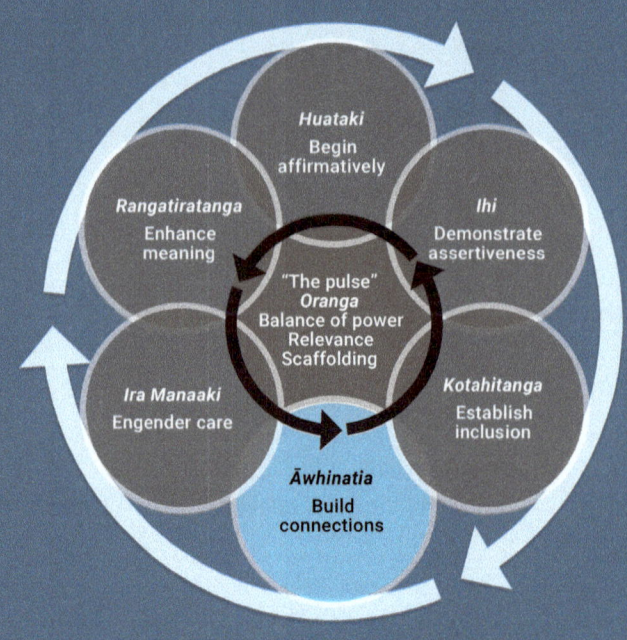

Outcomes and experiences

Draw connections together between kāinga, hapori, and kura

Tātaiako TāT TāWh
Our Code Our Standards PR DL

- Locate the learners in their world—tūrangawaewae.
- Learning experiences are cohesive, and explicit connections are made to other learning and the life of the learner.
- Put learners' individual needs at the centre of all learning experiences to ensure incorporating needs into context.
- Link the contexts of the home and of the school through whanaungatanga.
- Encourage tauira to talk about what happens in their lives, at home, in the classroom, and at the marae.
- Take or create opportunities for ākonga to go to the local marae to learn in context.

The connection between behaviour and the actions of others is a regular part of the curriculum

Tātaiako TāA TāM
Our Code Our Standards PR

- Mana-enhancing behaviour systems are understood and utilised.
- Model, acknowledge, and praise positive behaviour and interactions. Praise students for doing good and the right things.
- Clear expectations on behaviour and manaakitanga are taught and modelled.
- Ākonga and kaiako strive to understand one another and have mutual respect.

Ākonga are supported to lead learning	**Tātaiako TāA**
	Our Code Our Standards T LC

- 🟨 🟩 Students are guided to draw upon prior knowledge and use their strengths in teaching/learning opportunities.
- 🟨 🟩 Ākonga are purposefully taught and supported to lead others in learning.
- 🟨 🟩 Whānau are encouraged and supported to work alongside their tamaiti to support teaching and learning.
- 🟨 🟩 Those who exhibit a talent for leadership are encouraged to develop to realise potential.
- 🟨 🟩 Multiple forms of leadership are understood and nurtured.

Use a cyclical approach to teaching and managing the learning environment	**Tātaiako TāA**
	Our Code Our Standards T LC

- 🟨 🟩 Create opportunities to build on and reinforce prior knowledge, and develop skills to retain abilities over time. Model these expectations regularly and revisit them periodically.
- 🟨 🟩 Have clear routines that are easily followed by all.
- 🟨 🟩 Have high expectations around the way others are treated.
- 🟨 🟩 Draw on the environment/nature as a source of knowledge. For example, take students outdoors to study nature and attempt to make links with familiar whakataukī or pūrākau that draw on nature to convey wisdom. Revisit and link to these whakataukī periodically across the curriculum.
- 🟨 🟩 Revisit interventions as mana-enhancing teaching moments.
- 🟨 🟩 Be prepared with extension or modification steps to support optimisation of learning experiences.
- 🟨 🟩 Know your learners. Design tasks that challenge but create success. Recognise when tamariki are frustrated and figure out what they need from you: check-in support, explicit strategising, routine preemptive breaks, or time to change up the learning activity.

TUIA TE HERE TANGATA
Make meaningful human connections

Comments and self-reflection

Oranga: How am I embodying principles of **relevance**, **balance of power**, and **scaffolding** in the learning context? Improvements?

(Table cont. overleaf)

(Table cont. from previous page)

Where am I on the poutama?	What are my next steps?
☐ ☐ Mana Tangata—Empowering	
☐ ☐ Māramatanga—Embedding	
☐ ☐ Mātauranga—Exploring	
☐ ☐ Mōhiotanga—Encountering	
☐ ☐ Moemoeā—Envisioning	

[Follow-up date: __/__/____]
Have I met the goals above and how? What are my next steps now?

Additional readings

Castagno, A. E., & Brayboy, B. M. J. (2008). Culturally responsive schooling for indigenous youth: A review of the literature. *Review of Educational Research, 78*(4), 941–993. https://doi.org/10.3102/0034654308323036

Munford, R., & Sanders, J. (2011). Developing communities and enhancing participation in education In D. Bottrell & S. Goodwin (Eds.), *Schools, communities and social inclusion* (pp. 202–214). South Yarra, Vic: Palgrave Macmillan.

Ira Manaaki—Engender care

Ira Manaaki refers to building an ethos of care to support wellbeing, learning, and belonging. It promotes the development of positive attitudes towards self and learning. This includes having personal and cultural relevance in the learning experiences and allowing the ākonga choices and individual preference. Learners can see and feel their cultural values and perspectives within the learning context and content. Strive to make all interactions mana enhancing.

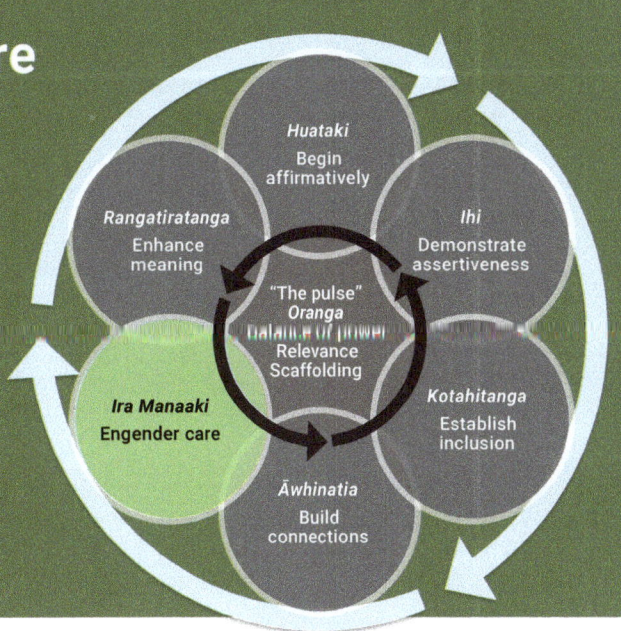

Outcomes and experiences

Tika, pono, and aroha are in all interactions

Tātaiako TaM TāWh
Our Code Our Standards LC

- Turn-taking, problem-solving, and choice-making are a common part of the learning process.
- Provide multiple ways and opportunities for learners to express themselves (e.g., stories, talks, conversations, whakaāhua visuals, personal inquiry projects, and whānau/learner hui or interactions).
- Learners are acknowledged at the day's beginning, after each learning experience, and at the end of the day.
- Promote opportunities for ākonga to express raru and mamae which are mana enhancing for all.
- Make time to discuss and reflect on learning and social experiences.
- Encourage acts of kindness by modelling and encouraging others to be kind; making them a visible part of everyday experiences.
- Inform whānau of successes so they can celebrate with their tamaiti. Keep whānau informed if there are concerns or ways for working through issues together.

Ākonga take responsibility for their own actions and wellbeing

Tātaiako TāA
Our Code Our Standards DL LC

- Encourage ākonga to draw on their own resources to make choices in the learning context.
- Model the acceptance of mistake-making by being open about your own limitations. Demonstrate growth mindsets by showing how mistakes and errors are opportunities for learning.
- Teach and promote self-regulation and goal setting (e.g., with step-by-step goals, and short- and long-term goals) for academic and social aspirations.
- Support learners to articulate and evaluate their learning.
- Support learners to identify and set next learning steps.

TOGETHER WEAVING THE REALISATION OF POTENTIAL

Rapport with ākonga and whānau is positive; kaiako are approachable in and outside the learning environment	*Tātaiako* TāWh
	Our Code Our Standards PR TW

- ☐ ☐ Explain learning and social needs proactively, patiently, and with kindness—put yourself in the shoes of the whānau.
- ☐ ☐ Get to know whānau, create partnerships. Bring good news, not just raru.
- ☐ ☐ Be aware of cultural idiosyncrasies (e.g., in language, eye contact, and body language).
- ☐ ☐ Be aware of perceptions, prejudices, power dynamics, and privilege. Be humble.

Caring for others is modelled, encouraged, and central to the kaupapa of the learning environment	*Tātaiako* TāM TāT
	Our Code Our Standards PR

- ☐ ☐ Open and close learning experiences with expressions of aroha and gratitude towards ākonga and their learning.
- ☐ ☐ Make time for learners to celebrate achievements with peers.
- ☐ ☐ Praise for positive behaviour, ignore minor infringements.
- ☐ ☐ Use pūrākau and whakataukī to exemplify values of manaaki and tiaki.

All support is mutual support: support is communal, collaborative, and shared	*Tātaiako* TāWh TāM
	Our Code Our Standards LC PL

- ☐ ☐ Encourage tauira to support the learning of others.
- ☐ ☐ Support the courage to try, as well as celebrating the success of the outcome.
- ☐ ☐ Support colleagues' learning and wellbeing.
- ☐ ☐ Participate in peer feedback—teach how to give positive feedback.
- ☐ ☐ Welcome relievers into the school and classroom.
- ☐ ☐ Support others, that contribute to the learning environment, to use systems (behaviour and reward) to support and promote positive learning experiences for all learners.

E KORE TE PUNA AROHA E MIMITI
Love is a spring that never runs dry

Comments and self-reflection

Oranga: How am I embodying principles of **relevance**, **balance of power**, and **scaffolding** in the learning context? Improvements?

MĀ TE WHIRITAHI, KA WHAKATUTUKI AI NGĀ PŪMANAWA Ā TĀNGATA

Where am I on the poutama?	What are my next steps?
☐ ☐ Mana Tangata—Empowering	
☐ ☐ Māramatanga—Embedding	
☐ ☐ Mātauranga—Exploring	
☐ ☐ Mōhiotanga—Encountering	
☐ ☐ Moemoeā—Envisioning	

[Follow-up date: __/__/____]

Have I met the goals above and how? What are my next steps now?

Additional readings

Berryman, M., Lawrence, D., & Lamont, R. (2018). Cultural relationships for responsive pedagogy: A bicultural mana ōrite perspective. *Set: Research Information for Teachers*(1), 3–10. https://doi.org/10.18296/set.0096

Cavanagh, T., Macfarlane, A., Glynn, T., & Macfarlane, S. (2012). Creating peaceful and effective schools through a culture of care. *Discourse: Studies in the Cultural Politics of Education, 33*(3), 443–455. https://doi.org/10.1080/01596306.2012.681902

Rangatiratanga— Enhance meaning

Rangatiratanga challenges and supports tamariki to achieve in physical, emotional, cognitive, social, spiritual, and cultural domains. Thinking and meaning-making are promoted. Learning is meaningful and connected to te ao Māori and to the life experiences of ākonga (home, whānau, community).

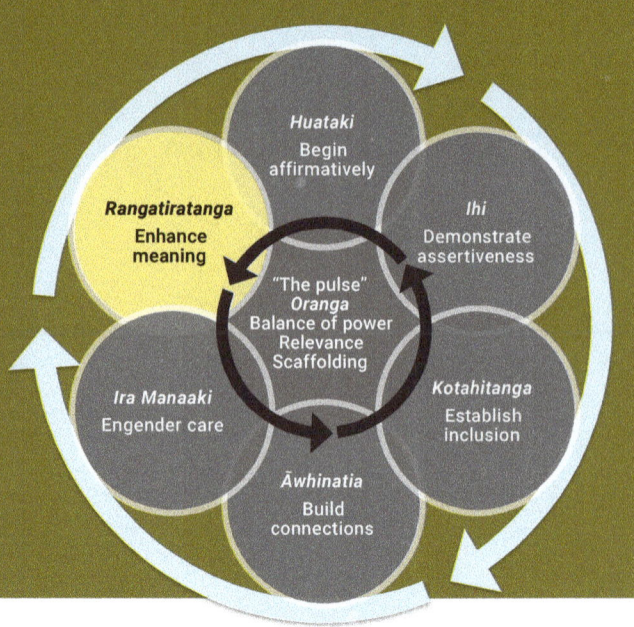

Outcomes and experiences

Ākonga exercise leadership over their own learning

Tātaiako TāT TāA
Our Code Our Standards TW DL

- ☐ ☐ Ākonga have opportunities to lead the learning experiences with support as needed.
- ☐ ☐ Acknowledge and utilise learner knowledge, strengths, and abilities within the learning environment.
- ☐ ☐ Kaiako don't need to dominate the learning environment.
- ☐ ☐ Ako, reciprocal learning and teaching, is part of the pedagogy.
- ☐ ☐ Tuakana–teina is part of the pedagogy.

Critical thinking develops through challenging and engaging learning

Tātaiako TāA TāW
Our Code Our Standards DL T

- ☐ ☐ Ask questions that encourage tauira to contribute and share their personal perspectives.
- ☐ ☐ Support learners to draw on knowledge of their own culture.
- ☐ ☐ Use open-ended questions to encourage and promote curiosity, problem-solving, inquiry, and exploration.
- ☐ ☐ All intentional teaching experiences have a specific and articulable purpose.
- ☐ ☐ Utilise local karakia, waiata, legends, stories, dance, and teaching resources that encourage all to kōrero Māori.

	Tātaiako TāA
Learners are supported to value self-determination, self-belief, and self-worth	Our Code Our Standards DL T

- ☐ ☐ Incorporate flexible planning and inquiry approaches that allow ākonga to direct the learning (ako).
- ☐ ☐ Encourage ākonga to overcome roadblocks in learning by building resilience behaviours (e.g., supporting peers to succeed, asking for help).
- ☐ ☐ Create opportunities for students to set their curriculum (e.g., What do you want to learn about? What interests you?)
- ☐ ☐ Design curriculum (lesson plan and learning environment) to support the development of characteristics of effective leadership (e.g., courage, generosity, community).
- ☐ ☐ Tauira understands themselves as learners. Teach and promote metacognition and other transferable skills that underpin learning.
- ☐ ☐ Each learner has opportunities to discuss strengths with kaiako and whānau (collaboration and student-led conferences).

	Tātaiako TāT
The cultural capital of ākonga Māori is evident in the learning context	Our Code Our Standards PR LC

- ☐ ☐ Encouraging student agency and sharing by utilising tuakana to guide teina. Include modelling, guidance, and practice opportunities.
- ☐ ☐ Cultivate respectful relationships with ākonga and respectful partnerships with whānau.
- ☐ ☐ Ensure active whānau involvement by creating opportunities for whānau in the learning environment.
- ☐ ☐ Give feedback that is purposeful, constructive, and acknowledges effort and achievement.

> **KO TE MANU E KAI ANA I TE MIRO, NŌNA TE NGAHERE. KO TE MANU E KAI ANA I TE MĀTAURANGA, NŌNA TE AO.**
>
> *The bird who partakes of the miro berry, inherits the forest. The bird who partakes of education, inherits the earth. (The exercise of agency leads to boundless opportunity).*

Comments and self-reflection

Oranga: How am I embodying principles of **relevance**, **balance of power**, and **scaffolding** in the learning context? Improvements?

(Table cont. overleaf)

(Table cont. from previous page)

Where am I on the poutama?	What are my next steps?
☐ ☐ Mana Tangata—Empowering	
☐ ☐ Māramatanga—Embedding	
☐ ☐ Mātauranga—Exploring	
☐ ☐ Mōhiotanga—Encountering	
☐ ☐ Moemoeā—Envisioning	

[Follow-up date: __/__/___]
Have I met the goals above and how? What are my next steps now?

Additional readings

Clarke, T., Macfarlane, S., & Macfarlane, A. (2018). Integrating indigenous Māori frameworks to ignite understandings within initial teacher education—and beyond (pp. 71–85). In P. Whitinui, M. a. d. C. Rodríguez, & O. McIvor (Eds.), *Promising practices in indigenous teacher education*. Singapore: Springer.

Penetito, W. (2009). Place-based education: catering for curriculum, culture and community. *New Zealand Annual Review of Education, 18*, 529

Engaging with whānau and hapori

The culturally responsive teaching and learning environment is a continuous, intentional act of co-creation that takes place in partnerships with ākonga, families and whānau: people, histories, identities, and culture are woven into the daily curriculum for learners journeying on their learning pathway. The partnership with whānau is infused in each of the preceding components. This section aims to support the building and sustaining of whānau relationships with staff and with the teaching and learning environment.

- Engage whānau in open dialogue about their tamariki.
- Establish trusting, personable, and respectful relationships with whānau.
- Work collaboratively towards a shared understanding of whānau perceptions, aspirations, and goals for their tamariki.

Engagements with whānau begin simply and grow organically through everyday interactions, through actively sharing personal and cultural histories and through the shared experience of ākonga developing and learning. Building strong, resilient connections requires effort to engage and to understand not only those you're seeking to connect with (looking outward) but also one's self (looking inward). Effective engagement is affective engagement (Dunstan, Hewitt & Tomaszewski, 2017); prioritise building emotional connections, sense of involvement and belonging, and shared purpose.

Whānau understand what and how their tamariki learn	Tātaiako TāWh
	Our Code Our Standards TW PR

- Provide frequent and constructive feedback about ākonga to whānau.
- Seek feedback from learners and from whānau about teaching and possible improvements.
- Take the time to talk with whānau, about anything.
- Relationships are built in shared time, laughter, etc. Celebrate learning with whānau.
- Meaningful hui with whānau to set goals and talk about learning.
- Seek whānau preference on contact methods (text message, phone call, email, kanohi ki te kanohi).
- Encourage whānau to speak, learn, embrace, and be proud of their Māoritanga.
- Show the school's commitment to uplifting learners' Māoritanga in meaningful and authentic ways.
- Whānau input is actively sought at all levels of school governance—with kaiako, Parent Teacher Association (PTA), and Board of Trustees.

Whānau participate in the delivery of learning	Tātaiako TāWh TāA
	Our Code Our Standards TW DL

- ☐ ☐ Utilise whānau members' expertise.
- ☐ ☐ Use reciprocal learning (ako) with ākonga Māori and their whānau.
- ☐ ☐ Collaborate with learners and whānau in areas they wish to know more about.
- ☐ ☐ Engage whānau to increase one's own knowledge of te reo Māori, te ao Māori, and tikanga Māori.
- ☐ ☐ Ask people to participate in the teaching and learning environment (e.g., whānau, community members)—show you value their skill and insight to build and grow the school's kaupapa.
- ☐ ☐ Koha is used appropriately to show appreciation for the whānau expertise that is utilised by the school.
- ☐ ☐ Invite whānau to share kai and kōrero.
- ☐ ☐ Actively seek ways to work with Māori whānau, whānau whānui, and hapori Māori.

Engaging others who are culturally dissimilar may require support to see and to understand other ways of making sense of the world and how whānau may see you as different from them (Gerlach, Browne & Greenwood, 2017). For example, engaging in cultural encounters challenge biases and assumptions (Campinha-Bacote, 2007) and provides opportunities to grow one's own understanding and perspective.

Meaningful engagements with whānau are actively sought by the school. These practices seek to create and maintain dialogue between school and ever-increasingly busy whānau. This informal dialogue may be unconventional in its pursuit; text messaging, with a coffee in the staffroom, a quick kōrero after the 3 pm bell or at the side of a sports ground. These conversations should be balanced between the celebration of achievements, and strategic planning for the promotion of positive behaviour and learning. They build rapport and trust which leads to productive partnerships for the co-constructing of learning (Kearney et al., 2014; Macfarlane, 2004, 2005).

The next steps ...

1. Using what you learn here to achieve a culturally inclusive learning environment.

2. Understand the identities, backgrounds, and cultures of learners in your learning community.

3. Consider how to facilitate cultural inclusivity using what you learned about motivating diverse learners and engaging them in their own learning.

4. Align and connect learners' home experiences and cultural values with those of the learning context.

Additional readings

Gerlach, A., Browne, A., & Greenwood, M. (2017). Engaging indigenous families in a community-based indigenous early childhood programme in British Columbia, Canada: A cultural safety perspective. *Health and Social Care Community, 25*(6), 1763–1773. https://doi.org/10.1111/hsc.12450

Karaka-Clarke, T. H. R. (2019). Pōwhiri : A ritual of encounter framework for engaging with whānau. *Set: Research Information for Teachers*, (1), 3–8. https://doi.org/10.18296/set.0135

Macfarlane, A. (2019, Winter). Engaging parents, whānau and hapori. *Ako: The journal for educational professionals*, 38.

Glossary of terms and phrases used in the text

Ako	Reciprocal teaching and learning
Ākonga	Student
Aroha	Love and compassion
Haere mai ki te kai/ whāriki	Come here to the food / mat
Hapori	A community
He māpuna te tamaiti	The dearness of the child
He wā kai	It is time/place for food
Hūmārie	Pleasant
Iwi	Kinship tribe
Kaiako	Teacher
Karakia	Prayer or acknowledgement
Kanohi ki te kanohi	Face to face
Kanohi kitea	The seen face
Kaupapa	Topic, subject or reason
Kei te pai ahau	I know what I'm doing
Koha	Gift or donation
Kōrero	Talk
Kaumātua,	Elder
Kuia	Woman elder
Mamae	Hurt or pain (not necessarily physical)
Mana	Status
Manaaki	Support, hospitality, or empowerment
Manaakitanga	Showing respect, generosity, support and care for others

Marae	A traditional site or complex of buildings
Mihi	Greeting
Ngākaunui	Commitment
Pepeha	Tribal saying, motto or formulaic expression
Pūrākau	Ancestral stories
Rangatira	A position of authority
Raru	A problem/s
Rauemi Aromatawai	Resource Assessment
Tamaiti	A child
Tamariki	Children
Tauira	Student
Te Ao Māori	The Māori Dimension
Tiaki	To care for
Tikanga	Correct procedure
Tuakana—teina	A teaching and learning concept: peer to peer, older to younger, younger to older, abled to less abled
Tūrangawaewae	A place where one has the right to stand and feels strong links to (usually through whakapapa)
Whāinga	Goals
Whakaeke	A process of entrance
Whakanuia	Celebrate
Whakapapa	Genealogy and kinship
Whakararanga mai	Line up
Whakataukī	Proverbial saying
Whakatika	Solution or preparation
Whakawhanaungatanga	A process of establishing relations, making connections, and relating well to others
Whānau	Family
Whanaungatanga	Relationships

Further useful readings

Huataki

Macfarlane, A., & Macfarlane S. (2011). Schooling as a cultural mission: Opening doorways for diverse learners. In D. Bottrell & S. Goodwin (Eds.), *Schools, communities and social inclusion* (pp. 108–124). Sydney, NSW: Palgrave Macmillan.

Macfarlane, S., Clarke, T., & Macfarlane, A. (2016) Language, literacy, identity and culture: Challenges and responses for indigenous learners. In L. Peer and G. Reid (Ed.), *Multilingualism, literacy and dyslexia: Breaking down barriers for educators* (2nd ed. pp. 120–128). Oxford, UK: Routledge.

Ihi

Macfarlane, A. (2004). *Kia hiwa rā! Listen to culture: Māori students' plea to educators.* Wellington: NZCER Press.

Macfarlane, A. (2011). Listening to culture—Māori principles and practices to support classroom management. In *Set: Research Information for Teachers. Māori Education Set Reprints*, pp. 6–19.

Kotahitanga

Graham, J.P.H. (2016, November). He Toka Tū Moana: Using notions of place to realise educational potential. Paper presented at The Politics of Learning NZARE conference, Wellington.

Macfarlane, S. (2015). Sociocultural contexts as enablers of diversity: Considerations for the primary years. In A. Macfarlane, S. Macfarlane & M. Webber. (Eds.), *Sociocultural realities: Exploring new horizons*, (pp. 100–116). Christchurch: Canterbury University Press.

Macfarlane, S., & Macfarlane, A. (2015). Inclusion for all—or just some? Drawing from evidence that counts for Māori: Whaia ki te ara tika. In M. Berryman, S. SooHoo, A. Nevin & T. Ford (Eds.), *Culture and relational inclusion: Contexts for becoming and belonging* (pp. 69–87). New York, NY: Peter Lang Publishing.

Āwhinatia

Duncan, W., Macfarlane, A., Quinlivan, K., & Macfarlane, S. (2016). Expanding on the meanings of empathy in the classroom: Seeing through a cultural lens. *Kairaranga Journal of Educational Practice*, 17(2), 3–13.

Glynn, T., Cowie, B., Cass, K. & Macfarlane, A. (2010). Culturally responsive pedagogy: Connecting New Zealand teachers of science with their Māori students. *The Australian Journal of Indigenous Education*, 39, pp. 118–127.

Kounin, J. (1977). *Discipline and group management in classrooms* (Rev. Ed.). New York, NY: Holt Renhart Winston.

Ira manaaki

Glynn, T., Cavanagh, T., Macfarlane, A., & Macfarlane, S. (2011). Listening to culture. In V. Margrain & A. Macfarlane, (Eds.). *Responsive pedagogy: Engaging restoratively with challenging behaviour* (pp. 46–63). Wellington: NZCER Press.

Rangatiratanga

Macfarlane, A., & Prochnow, J. (2011). Student behaviour: Towards a theoretical understanding. In V. Margrain and A. Macfarlane (Eds.), *Responsive pedagogy: Engaging restoratively with challenging behaviour* (pp. 27–45).Wellington: NZCER Press.

Macfarlane, A. (2010). An educultural approach to classroom management: Integrating body mind and heart. *New Zealand Physical Educator*, 43(1), pp. 7–11.

Oranga

Cavanagh, T., Macfarlane, A., Glynn, T. & Macfarlane, S. (2012). Creating peaceful and effective schools through a culture of care. *Discourse: Cultural Politics of Education*, 33(4), pp. 1–13.

Macfarlane, S., & Derby, M. (2018). From the rākau to the ngākau: Exploring authentic approaches to leadership, policy, and pedagogy. *Ipu Kererū: Blog of the New Zealand Association for Research in Education (NZARE)*. https://nzareblog.wordpress.com/2018/04/26/rakau-ngakau/

Engaging Whānau

Macfarlane, S. (2015). Sociocultural contexts as enablers of diversity: Considerations for the primary years. In Macfarlane, A. H., Macfarlane, S., & Webber, M. (eds), *Sociocultural realities: exploring new horizons* (pp. 100–116). Christchurch: Canterbury University Press.

References

Campinha-Bacote, J. (2007). *The process of cultural competence in the delivery of healthcare services: A culturally competent model of care* (5th ed.). Cincinnati, OH: Transcultural C.A.R.E. Associates.

Dunstan, L., Hewitt, B., & Tomaszewski, W. (2017). Indigenous children's affective engagement with school: The influence of sociocultural, subjective and relational factors. *Australian Journal of Education*, 6(3), 250–269.

Education Council. (2017). *Our code our standards: Code of professional responsibility and standards for the teaching profession / Ngā tikanga matatika ngā paerewa: Ngā tikanga matatika mō te haepapa ngaiotanga me ngā paerewa mō te umanga whakaakoranga*. Wellington: Author.

Education Review Office. (2016). *School evaluation indicators: Effective practice for improvement and learner success*. Wellington: Author.

Gerlach, A., Browne, A., & Greenwood, M. (2017). Engaging indigenous families in a community-based indigenous early childhood programme in British Colombia, Canada: A cultural safety perspective. *Health and Social Care Community*, 25(6), 1763-1773. https://doi.org/10.1111/hsc.12450

Glasser, W. (1992). *Quality school: Managing students without coercion*. New York, NY: Harper Perennial.

Hahunga, Hami "*The Hikairo Rationale.*" Received by Angus Macfarlane, 24 September 1997.

Kearney, E., McIntosh, L., Perry, B., Dockett, S., & Clayton, K. (2014). Building positive relationships with indigenous children, families and communities: Learning at the cultural interface. *Critical Studies in Education*, 55(3), 338–352.

Kounin, J. (1977). *Discipline and group management in classrooms* (Rev. Ed.). New York, NY: Holt Renhart Winston.

Macfarlane, A. (2004). *Kia hiwa rā! Listen to culture: Māori learners' plea to educators.* Wellington: NZCER Press.

Macfarlane, A. (2005). Inclusion and Māori ecologies: As educultural approach. In D. Fraser, R. Moltzen & K. Ryba (Eds.), *Learners with special needs in Aotearoa New Zealand* (3rd ed., pp. 99–116). Melbourne, Vic: Thomson Dunmore Press.

Macfarlane, A., Macfarlane, S. & Webber, M. (Eds.) (2015). *Sociocultural realities: Exploring new horizons.* Christchurch: Canterbury University Press.

Macfarlane, A., & Macfarlane, S., Teirney, S., Kuntz, J.R., Rarere-Briggs, B., Currie, M., Gibson, M. & Macfarlane, R. (2019). *The Hikairo Schema: Culturally responsive teaching and learning in early childhood settings.* Wellington: NZCER Press.

Mead, S. M., & Grove, N. (2001). *Ngā pēpeha a ngā tīpuna: The sayings of the ancestors.* Wellington: Victoria University Press.

Ministry of Education. (2007). *The New Zealand curriculum.* Wellington: Learning Media.

Ministry of Education. (2008). *Te marautanga o Aotearoa.* Wellington: Learning Media.

Ministry of Education, & New Zealand Teachers Council. (2011). *Tātaiako: Cultural competencies for teachers of Māori learners.* Wellington: Author.

Pere, R. (1982). *Ako: Concepts and learning in the Māori tradition.* Hamilton, Department of Sociology, University of Waikato. Reprinted 1994. Te Kohanga Reo Trust. Wellington.

Riley, M. (2013), *Wise words of the Māori: Revealing history and traditions.* Paraparaumu, NZ: Viking Seven Seas.

Stafford, D. (1967). *Te Arawa: A history of the Arawa people.* Auckland: Reed Publishing.

www.ingramcontent.com/pod-product-compliance
Lightning Source LLC
Chambersburg PA
CBHW061548010526
44114CB00027B/2961